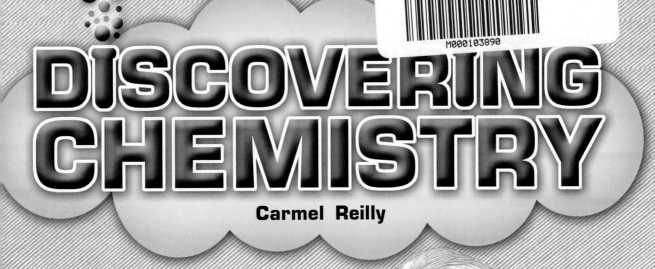

DISCOVERING CHEMISTRY

Carmel Reilly

Rigby®

www.Rigby.com
1-800-531-5015

Rigby Focus Forward

This Edition © 2009 Rigby, a Harcourt Education Imprint

Published in 2008 by Nelson Australia Pty Ltd ACN: 058 280 149
A Cengage Learning company

2 3 4 5 6 7 8 374 14 13 12 11 10 09 08
Printed and bound in China

Discovering Chemistry
ISBN-13   978-1-4190-3847-1
ISBN-10   1-4190-3847-8

Acknowledgments
The author and publisher would like to acknowledge permission to reproduce material
from the following sources:
Photographs by Corbis/ Photolibrary, back cover, pp. 3, 5; Thinkstock, p. 13b; Fotolia,
p. 7b; iStockphoto, pp. 4a-d, 12a-b, 23a-c; Mary Evans Picture Library, p. 7a; Newspix/
Gregg Porteous, p. 22; Photolibrary/Carol and Mike Werner, p. 18/ Lebrecht Music &
Arts Photo Library, p. 9/ Novosti Novosti, p. 16/ Science Photo Library, pp. 9 inset, 13a,
15a, 15c, 17/ Sheila Terry/SPL, cover, pp. 1, 6, 14a/ STE, p. 11/ The Bridgeman Art Library,
p. 8/ Science Photo Library, pp. 10, 12c-d, 21b/ Andrew Lambert Photography, pp. 15b,
15d/ E.R. Degginger, p. 21a/ John Greim, p. 5 inset.

DISCOVERING CHEMISTRY

Carmel Reilly

Contents

Chapter 1

INTRODUCING CHEMISTRY

Plants, animals, humans, and even everyday things are all made up of a combination of substances. These substances are called elements. Chemistry is the branch of science that studies the elements—what things are made of and how they can change.

chemists

Scientists who study chemistry are called chemists. They **investigate** what makes up substances and how they react under different conditions. Chemists are also interested in finding ways to make new substances and materials.

Chapter 2

BEGINNINGS OF CHEMISTRY

For thousands of years, people have wondered what things are made from. People in ancient India and ancient Greece believed that everything was made from only four elements:

- air
- earth
- fire
- water

men in ancient Greece

People in ancient China believed there were actually five elements:

- air
- earth
- fire
- water
- metal

people in ancient China

The Chinese thought these things were elements because they seemed to be what all other materials and substances were made from. For example, Chinese people made pottery by mixing earth and water together and then heating them by fire.

For many centuries, people continued to believe there were only four or five elements. But during the Middle Ages (500 A.D. to 1500 A.D.), some people started to investigate the nature of substances to see whether this was the case.

Other people experimented with turning ordinary metals into gold. This practice became known as alchemy. Alchemists never managed to create gold, but they developed a good knowledge of chemical substances and chemical reactions. They also invented tools, such as funnels, strainers, and scales, that were later used in chemistry.

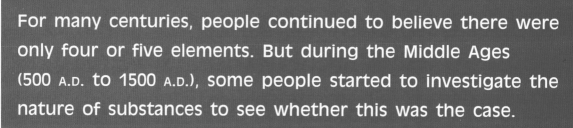

scales

an alchemist

Louis Pasteur at work in his laboratory

chemists Otto Hahn and Lise Mietner

In the last 200 years, chemists have performed experiments revealing that not everything is made only from the elements of air, earth, fire, water, and metal.

Chapter 3

THE BEGINNING OF MODERN CHEMISTRY

During the 1600s, scientists began to understand more about the makeup of materials and substances through experimenting. Scientists began to see that air, earth, fire, and water were not elements themselves but were made up of other elements.

Jean Baptiste van Helmont (1579–1644) a Belgian doctor and chemist

Robert Boyle

One of the first scientists to realize that there were many elements was Robert Boyle (1627–1691). Boyle is known today as the father of modern chemistry. He believed that experiments and observations were the only way to find out about the world.

Boyle did many experiments with air. These experiments showed that air was not an element itself but was made up of other smaller elements.

Elements and Atoms

Everything is made from tiny particles called atoms. An element is a substance that is made of only one type of atom—a substance in its purest form. We now know today that there are more than 100 elements, and about 80 percent of them are metals, such as gold, copper, and iron.

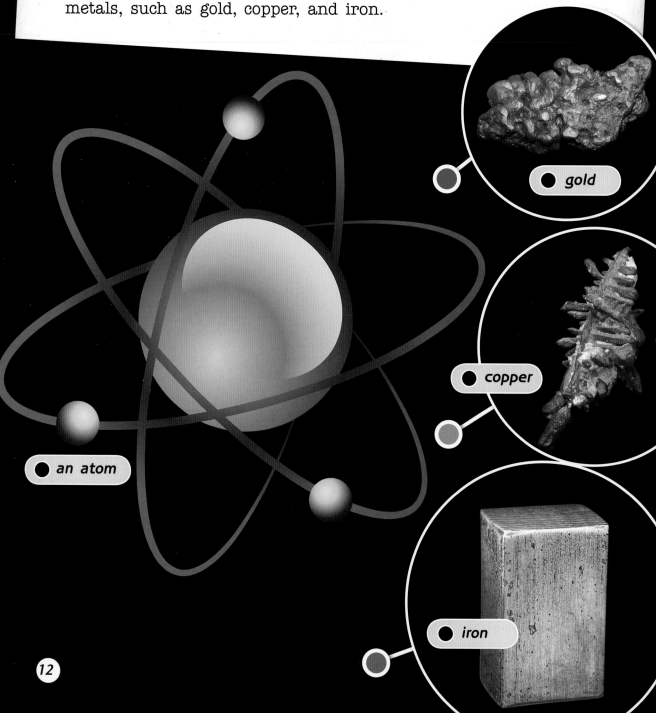

gold

copper

an atom

iron

Henry Cavendish

NITROGEN

Oxygen

Hydrogen

Throughout the 1700s and 1800s, scientists made more advances in chemistry. Henry Cavendish (1731–1810) was able to make water when doing an experiment with air. From this he saw that water had to be made up of more than one element and that water and air had elements in common. This experiment also led Cavendish to discover the element hydrogen. Around the same time, other chemists discovered oxygen and nitrogen.

A little later, the French chemist Antoine Lavoisier (1743–1794) was the first to show that air was a mixture of elements. He also proved that water is a compound of oxygen and hydrogen. Lavoisier wrote the first modern chemistry book and started the system of naming elements.

Antoine Lavoisier

125 ml

H_2O

water

Humphry Davy (1778–1829) found a way to split compounds using an **electric current**. He also discovered a number of elements, including sodium and calcium. Around the same time, John Dalton (1766–1844) put forward the idea that everything is made of atoms and that each element contains only one kind of atom.

Humphry Davy

John Dalton

calcium

sodium

Compounds and Mixtures

A compound is a substance that is made up of more than one element joined together chemically. An example of a compound is pure water. It is made up of the elements hydrogen and oxygen.

A mixture is made up of more than one substance. An example of a mixture is air. It is made up of elements such as oxygen and compounds such as carbon dioxide.

Chapter 4

THE PERIODIC TABLE

By the 1860s, scientists had discovered 63 elements, each of which had been given an **atomic number**. A Russian scientist, Dmitry Mendeleyev (1843–1907), used these numbers to help design a table for the elements. He called this the periodic table. Making this table helped him and other scientists to understand the connections between each element and to see how the elements could combine to make up different substances.

● *Dmitry Mendeleyev*

Typische

H = 1

Typische

H = 1

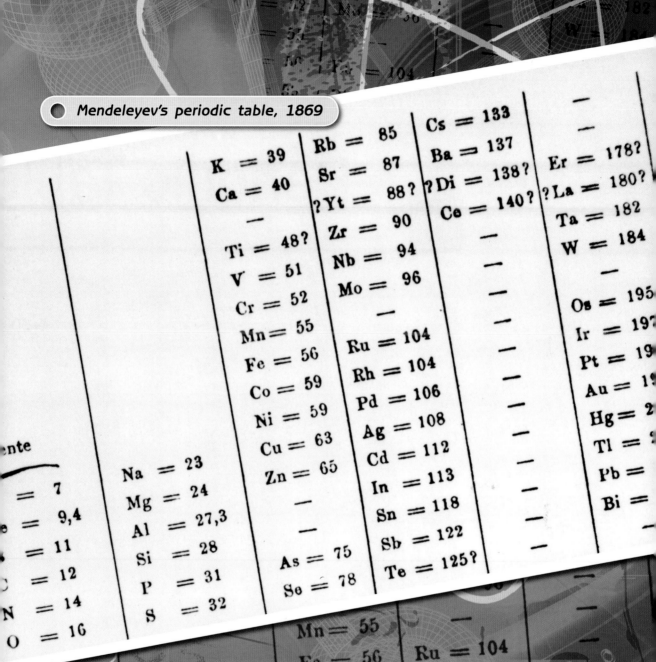

Mendeleyev's periodic table, 1869

Ti = 48?
V = 51
Cr = 52
Mn = 55
Fe = 56
Co = 59
Ni = 59
Cu = 63
Zn = 65

K = 39
Ca = 40
—

Rb = 85
Sr = 87
?Yt = 88?
Zr = 90
Nb = 94
Mo = 96
—
Ru = 104
Rh = 104
Pd = 106
Ag = 108
Cd = 112
In = 113
Sn = 118
Sb = 122
Te = 125?

Cs = 133
Ba = 137
?Di = 138?
Ce = 140?
—
—
—
—
—
—
—
—
—
—
—
—

—
—
Er = 178?
?La = 180?
Ta = 182
W = 184
—
Os = 195
Ir = 19?
Pt = 19
Au = 1?
Hg = 2
Tl = ?
Pb =
Bi =

Na = 23
Mg = 24
Al = 27,3
Si = 28
P = 31
S = 32

As = 75
Se = 78

ente
= 7
e = 9,4
= 11
= 12
N = 14
O = 16

Mn = 55
Fe = 56
Ru = 104

In addition Mendeleyev discovered a number of new elements, which he added to the table. He also predicted some other elements, which were not known then but have been discovered since!

The periodic table lists all the known elements. Some of these were discovered centuries ago, while others have only been discovered in the last few years.

Periodic Table

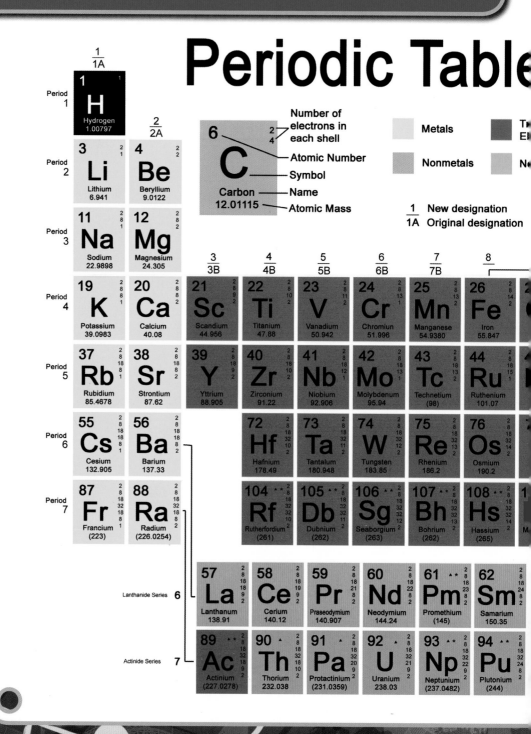

of the Elements

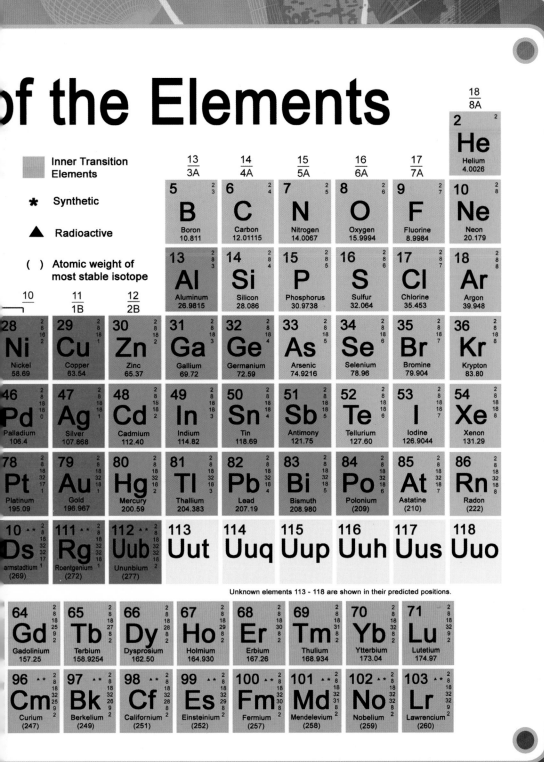

Inner Transition Elements

* Synthetic

▲ Radioactive

( ) Atomic weight of most stable isotope

18 / 8A
2 2
He
Helium
4.0026

13 / 3A	14 / 4A	15 / 5A	16 / 6A	17 / 7A	
5 2,3	6 2,4	7 2,5	8 2,6	9 2,7	10 2,8
B	**C**	**N**	**O**	**F**	**Ne**
Boron	Carbon	Nitrogen	Oxygen	Fluorine	Neon
10.811	12.01115	14.0067	15.9994	8.9984	20.179
13 2,8,3	14 2,8,4	15 2,8,5	16 2,8,6	17 2,8,7	18 2,8,8
Al	**Si**	**P**	**S**	**Cl**	**Ar**
Aluminum	Silicon	Phosphorus	Sulfur	Chlorine	Argon
26.9815	28.086	30.9738	32.064	35.453	39.948

10	11 / 1B	12 / 2B						
28 2,8,16,2	29 2,8,18,1	30 2,8,18,2	31 2,8,18,3	32 2,8,18,4	33 2,8,18,5	34 2,8,18,6	35 2,8,18,7	36 2,8,18,8
Ni	**Cu**	**Zn**	**Ga**	**Ge**	**As**	**Se**	**Br**	**Kr**
Nickel	Copper	Zinc	Gallium	Germanium	Arsenic	Selenium	Bromine	Krypton
58.69	63.54	65.37	69.72	72.59	74.9216	78.96	79.904	83.80
46 2,8,18,18	47 2,8,18,18	48 2,8,18,18	49 2,8,18,18	50 2,8,18,18	51 2,8,18,18	52 2,8,18,18	53 2,8,18,18	54 2,8,18,18
Pd	**Ag**	**Cd**	**In**	**Sn**	**Sb**	**Te**	**I**	**Xe**
Palladium	Silver	Cadmium	Indium	Tin	Antimony	Tellurium	Iodine	Xenon
106.4	107.868	112.40	114.82	118.69	121.75	127.60	126.9044	131.29
78 2,8,18,32,17	79 2,8,18,32,18,1	80 2,8,18,32,18,2	81 2,8,18,32,18,3	82 2,8,18,32,18,4	83 2,8,18,32,18,5	84 2,8,18,32,18,6	85 2,8,18,32,18,7	86 2,8,18,32,18,8
Pt	**Au**	**Hg**	**Tl**	**Pb**	**Bi**	**Po**	**At**	**Rn**
Platinum	Gold	Mercury	Thallium	Lead	Bismuth	Polonium	Astatine	Radon
195.09	196.967	200.59	204.383	207.19	208.980	(209)	(210)	(222)
10 ▲* 2,8,18,32,17	111 ▲* 2,8,18,32,18,1	112 ▲* 2,8,18,32,18,2	113 **Uut**	114 **Uuq**	115 **Uup**	116 **Uuh**	117 **Uus**	118 **Uuo**
Ds	**Rg**	**Uub**						
Darmstadtium 1	Roentgenium 1	Ununbium 2						
(269)	(272)	(277)						

Unknown elements 113 - 118 are shown in their predicted positions.

64 2,8,18,25,9,2	65 2,8,18,27,8,2	66 2,8,18,28,8,2	67 2,8,18,29,8,2	68 2,8,18,30,8,2	69 2,8,18,31,8,2	70 2,8,18,32,8,2	71 2,8,18,32,9,2
Gd	**Tb**	**Dy**	**Ho**	**Er**	**Tm**	**Yb**	**Lu**
Gadolinium	Terbium	Dysprosium	Holmium	Erbium	Thulium	Ytterbium	Lutetium
157.25	158.9254	162.50	164.930	167.26	168.934	173.04	174.97
96 ▲* 2	97 ▲* 2	98 ▲* 2	99 ▲* 2	100 ▲* 2	101 ▲* 2	102 ▲* 2	103 ▲* 2
Cm	**Bk**	**Cf**	**Es**	**Fm**	**Md**	**No**	**Lr**
Curium	Berkelium	Californium 2	Einsteinium 2	Fermium	Mendelevium	Nobelium	Lawrencium
(247)	(249)	(251)	(252)	(257)	(258)	(259)	(260)

Chapter 5

SOME OF THE ELEMENTS

Iron	Platinum	Phosphorus
symbol: Fe	symbol: Pt	symbol: P
discovered in ancient times	discovered in the **pre-Columbian** era	discovered in 1669 by Hennig Brand
used for tools, ornaments, and weapons now used in car manufacturing and structural parts for buildings	used in jewelry, laboratory equipment, and dentistry	used in detergents and fertilizers

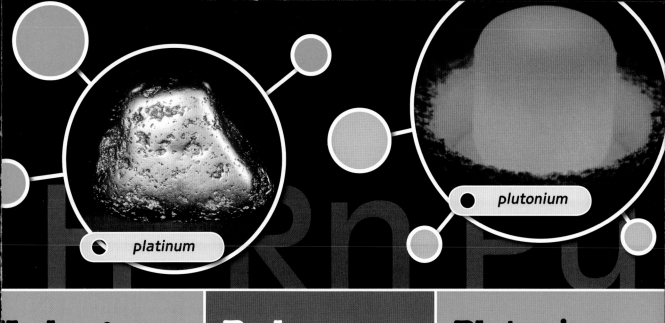

platinum

plutonium

Hydrogen	Radon	Plutonium
symbol: H	symbol: Rn	symbol: Pu
discovered in 1766 by Henry Cavendish	discovered in 1898 by Fredrich Ernst Dorn	discovered in 1940 by G.T. Seaborg
used in balloons and metal refining	used in the treatment of cancer	used in bombs and nuclear reactors

H Rn Pu

Chapter 6

CHEMISTRY TODAY

Without chemistry and all the chemists who have investigated and created new substances, the world today would be a very different place.

By understanding how elements combine and what substances are made of, chemists have been able to work out how to make thousands of new and useful products, such as synthetic fabrics, LCD and plasma computer and TV screens, paints, sunscreen, cosmetics, and medicines.

Glossary

atomic number   a number that identifies an element. It is the number of protons found in the nucleus of an atom.

electric current   a flow of electricity

investigate   to carry out research into something

pre-Columbian   the era before and during Christopher Columbus' first landing in the Americas, in 1492

Index